Divorce Devotions: 30 Days of Healing for a Broken

Andrea M. Stuckey

Copyright © 2021 Andrea M. Stuckey

All rights reserved.

DEDICATION

To every divorced woman whose heart has been broken into a million pieces, yet still desire true authentic healing. You inspire me to continue on purpose to provide resources to help you heal and create a beautiful, new life.

INTRODUCTION

Divorce is an overwhelming life transition. It can cause immense feelings and thoughts about various areas of your life. As a divorce coach, I have coached and consulted with countless women who have been challenged with the topics and areas covered in this book.

This devotional is designed to encourage you, yet provoke you towards deep thought and insight for yourself. Self-honesty is the beginning to journey of healing. The journey of divorce is a very personal one and requires a great deal of introspection to get to a place of a healed heart along with a happy and free life.

Feel free to use this devotion in the way that is right for you. You can read and focus on one devotion or topic per week, where you give yourself ample time to work through the questions or activities. You can also read a devotion per day or randomly pick topics that are applicable for your life right now. The choice is yours.

As challenging as divorce is, it is not the end all be all for your life. At times it will feel like that, but know that God is with you along your journey of healing and change. He will strengthen you and give you what you need when you need it. Seek Him in every decision that you must make, and allow His peace to prevail in your life.

There is so much more life to live. You can live and love again.
-Andrea M. Stuckey

CONTENTS

1 When Life Changes

2 Feeling Failure

3 Ditching Denial

4 What About My Children?

5 Finding Your Personal Freedom

6 Make Yourself A Priority

7 The Danger Of Pride

8 Who's In Your Inner Circle?

9 Beware Of Bitterness

10 Don't Suffer In Silence

11 Rediscover Love For Yourself

12 Detecting Red Flags

13 What's Your Next Step?

14 Mask Off!

15 A Victim No More!

16 Who Will You Become

17 Do You Know Your Value?

18 Adjust Your Focus.

19 Are You Ready To Trust Again?

20 The Co-parenting Blues

21 Some Things Must Go

22 Rejection Is Real

23 Loneliness vs Singleness

24 Fighting Forgiveness

25	The Angst Of Anger
26	The Will To Be Well
27	Your Mindset Matters
28	Check Your Environment
29	Fostering New Friendships
30	Acceptance, The Final Frontier

Divorce Devotions

1. When Life Changes.

"This is my command—be strong and courageous! Do not be afraid or discouraged. For the Lord, your God is with you wherever you go." -Joshua 1:9 NLT

Divorce changes lives. Your life may be changing. Changing in a way that you may not understand. You may be wondering how you got to this place and trying to imagine what is next for you.

When you are going through a period where unfamiliar change is occurring, it is imperative that you get clarity on what is currently happening in every area of your life. Once you thoroughly assess your life, and you understand where you are, you begin to have a position of power and strength even during change.

Identify your positive and negative feelings/concerns in your 5 life zones: spiritually, emotionally, socially, financially, and occupationally.

Example: Emotionally- positive; I finally feel free and in a peaceful environment. Negative; I cannot seem to control my anger.

Once completed, write a prayer to God about the areas of your challenges. Expect and listen for his direction. Meanwhile, focus your energies on the positive areas of your life every day. As God reveals direction, be sure to act.

NOTES

2. Feeling Failure

"My flesh and my heart faileth: but God is the strength of my heart, and my portion forever." -Psalms 73:26 KJV

Your marriage may have failed, but YOU are not a failure. God still loves and values you. Mistakes are a part of life and the awareness and admission of those mistakes are a part of growth. Keep moving forward towards the fulfilling life that you desire and deserve.

List 3 mistakes that YOU made in your marriage. Besides each mistake, share what you could have done differently.

1._____

_____

2._____

_____

3._____

_____

NOTES

3. Ditching Denial

"The simple believe everything, but the prudent gives thought to his steps."

-Proverbs 14:15 (NLT)

It seems unimaginable. No one really plans to get a divorce, so when you are faced with the unexpected, it is easy to pretend that it is not really happening. Repeatedly in your mind, you may replay the early days of the relationship. How did you get to this point? Now you are here. There are emotions to identify and work through, and necessary life tasks that must be taken care of. Wherever you are on your journey, it is imperative that you are honest and open with yourself as to what has happened and where you currently are. Once you begin to face the truth, you can begin to move forward, set various goals, and begin a journey of healing.

What season are you in on your divorce journey?
<1year, 1-3years, 4+ years.

What emotional state are you most of the time? Why?

_____

_____

NOTES

4. What about the children?

"Teach them to your children. Talk about them when you are at home and when you are on the road, when you are going to bed and when you are getting up."
-Deuteronomy 11:19 NLT

One of the biggest concerns that you face during a divorce is the outcome of any children involved. You wonder how this experience will shape and mold their lives. You may have even stayed in a negative environment longer than you should have because you were unsure of the effects that divorce would have on the children.

There are two vital points to remember when children are involved in divorce.

1. Children need both parents. It really does not matter how you feel about your ex. It really does not matter what your ex-has or has not done to you, or what you have done to them. Children love and need both of their parents in very different ways. Unless the children will be in danger, they need time with the other parent, and you should advocate for that right even if the other parent is not aware of that need. If you cannot agree on

visitation, then there are court supported services that can help.

2. Begin with the end in mind. Co-parenting requires a great deal of emotional maturity from the parents. Think about the relationship that you want your children to have with the other parent 10 years from now. Weddings, births, teenage years, and celebratory moments. How will your children feel then if the other parent would be absent? What role will you play in making those future years and bonds healthy with the other parent?

Name three ways that you can help your children build bonds with the other parent.

1._____

2._____

3._____

NOTES

5. Finding Your Personal Freedom

So, Christ has truly set us free. Now make sure that you stay free, and do not get tied up again in the slavery to the law. - Galatians 5:1 NLT

Freedom is the power or right to act, speak or think as one wants without hindrance or restraint.

Divorce is much more than being "free" from an unhappy marriage that has ended. Post-divorce is about finding out who are you now. During your marriage were you free to be authentically you? Were you living a life or a lie? Did you allow all your personal dreams, goals, and aspirations to die?

Oftentimes, you may have been carrying emotional hurts and wounds that led you to behave unseemly in relationships. Codependency, anger, insecurities, and abuse are to name a few.

Now that you are out of a relationship that could have been restrictive to you in many ways, how can you begin to find your own personal freedom?

Answer the following questions.

1. Have you been carrying any emotional hurts from previous relationships or childhood? List *at least* one.

_____

_____

2. What are some possible ways that you can begin to work on those hurts or seek help to begin a journey of personal freedom?

_____

_____

Now, act on one of those ways. Start now! You are worth beginning your journey to freedom.

NOTES
_____

6. Make Yourself A Priority

"Don't you realize that your body is the temple of the Holy Spirit, who lives in you and was given to you by God? You do not belong to yourself, for God bought you with a high price. So, you must honor God with your body." -1 Corinthians 6:19-20

With all the major transitions of a divorce, you may wonder how you can make time for yourself. Yes, the emotions are a rollercoaster and there are physical tasks to be done, paperwork to fill out, attorneys to contact, court dates to fulfill and possibly children to co-parent. Therefore, it is vital that you make yourself a priority and find times to refresh and regroup. If you do not you will inevitably burn out.

Some signs of burnout include but are not limited to insomnia, chronic fatigue, inability to concentrate, headaches, chest pain, and loss of appetite. If you currently suffer from any of these symptoms, it may be an indicator that you need to refocus and begin to implement a few ways to de-stress, relax and laugh. Yes, laugh.

You can laugh even if you are going through a divorce. It is important that you seek out environments and people who love and support you during this time. Watching a great comedy, taking a bubble bath, reading a good book or going on a simple walk can help minimize the stresses of divorce.

List three ways that you will commit to yourself to help you steer clear of burnout.

List the activity, day, and time of your commitment.

1. _____

2. _____

3. _____

NOTES

7. The Danger of Pride

This is what the Lord says: "Don't let the wise boast in their wisdom, or the powerful boast in their power, or the rich boast in their riches. But those who wish to boast should boast in this alone: that they truly know me and understand that I am the Lord who demonstrates unfailing love and who brings justice and righteousness to the earth and that I delight in these things. I, the Lord, have spoken! - Jeremiah 9:23-24 NLT

Pride has damaged and destroyed many marriages and relationships. Pride is the quality of having an excessively high opinion of oneself or one's importance, or arrogance. In relationships, pride can be strong enough to prevent someone from apologizing, admitting faults, encouraging one another, being vulnerable and honest.

Healthy relationships are built on trust, honesty, commitment, and communication. When pride is at the forefront of relationships, it is difficult to operate in those principles.

Can you recall areas of pride in your former relationships? List them.

_____
_____
_____
_____
_____

Where do you think your prideful moments originated?

_____
_____
_____
_____
_____

NOTES

8. Who is in Your Inner Circle?

Oh, the joys of those who do not follow the advice of the wicked, or stand around with sinners, or join in with mockers, but they delight in the law of the Lord, meditating on it day and night. -Psalms 1:1-2 NLT

As you navigate your divorce journey, your circle of people and associations will play a major key in your healing. When you surround yourself with people who generally love and support you, you have an environment love and encouragement. Those are helping you move forward in a variety of ways; they will also tell you the truth in love. If you surround yourself with negative people who constantly assist you in rehashing the old, blaming others, and have no encouraging words for you, you will remain in a state of stagnation and pain. Healing from a divorce is a process, and there are stages you will go through. However, you should be generally progressing over time. If you are not, I suggest that you really begin to assess your circle of people whom you communicate with on a regular basis. Listen to the tone and content of those conversations.

How do you feel after those conversations?

Name three people or groups that you spend a lot of time with. Write down a positive trait that they add to your life in this season. If you cannot identify a positive trait, perhaps you may want to think of minimizing that contact as you are healing and rebuilding your life.

1._____

_____

2._____

_____

3._____

_____

NOTES

9. Beware of Bitterness

"Look after each other so that none of you fails to receive the grace of God. Watch out that no poisonous root of bitterness grows up to trouble you, corrupting many. Make sure that no one is immoral or godless like Esau, who traded his birthright as the firstborn son for a single meal. You know that afterward when he wanted his father's blessing, he was rejected. It was too late for repentance, even though he begged with bitter tears."

- Hebrews 12: 15-17 (NIV)

Anger is the most prevalent emotion in most divorces. It is the most difficult emotion to control and release. The causes of the anger vary from feeling rejected, betrayed, and overwhelmed, to blaming, feeling like a failure and a host of other origins. Anger is an emotion. It is neither good nor bad. It is what we do with the anger that matters. Firstly, it is important that you identify the anger for what it is. There is not a need to repress it. Being honest and identifying your anger is a powerful step in your healing process. Next, you must deal with the reasons that you feel the anger. Finally, at some point (not overnight) you must release the anger.

If you do not release the anger over a period, your anger will turn into bitterness.

Roots of bitterness come from unforgiveness and can lead to resentment. We create "roots" based on the judgments that we make against others. That bitterness develops a root and then becomes very difficult to uproot and release.

Unreleased anger has spiritual manifestations as well as physical manifestations. Spiritually, unreleased anger shows up in a personality weight of sarcasm, moodiness, easily offended, and a difficulty being vulnerable in relationships. Physically, unreleased anger can show up in anxiety, depression, heart palpitations, chest pain, heart problems, and autoimmune diseases.

Do not allow your anger to turn into bitterness. Forgive, release, and move forward in your life. You will gain a great deal of freedom.

Answer the following questions:

1. Who are you are angry at?

_____
_____
_____
_____
_____

2. What caused your anger?

_____
_____
_____
_____

3. Do you want to forgive them? Why or why not?

_____
_____
_____
_____
_____

4. Read the Prayer of Forgiveness located in the back of this book.

NOTES

10. Do not suffer in silence.

Then Jesus said, "Come to me, all of you who are weary and carry heavy burdens, and I will give you rest. Take my yoke upon you. Let me teach you because I am humble and gentle at heart, and you will find rest for your souls. For my yoke is easy to bear, and the burden I give you is light." - Matthew 11:28-30

The unbearable rollercoaster of emotions may have you in a very surprising emotional space. Perhaps you have not even told anyone about your pending or past divorce for fear of isolation, or judgment. You may be just going through the process in silence and alone. This is one of the best ways to thwart your healing and your recovery.

No man is an island, and when you are going through such an emotionally challenging time of pain and transition you need to be around people who love and support you. There are others who may be going through a similar life change and can empathize with you. When you isolate yourself, you open the door to greater chances of chronic anxiety, depression, and grief.

There's power and strength in numbers. If you have not already, seek out a local divorce support group.

There are also a host of online communities as well to share your challenges and experiences with others. You can also go to a Pastor, Christian mentor, therapist, or a life coach. All these options will assist you in your healing as you navigate your divorce journey.

Identify three types of support that you could potentially communicate with to assist you emotionally through your divorce healing.

1._____

2._____

3._____

NOTES

We must let go of the life that we have planned, to accept the one that is waiting for us.

-Joseph Campbell

———————————————

11. Rediscover love for yourself.

"Love your neighbor as yourself."- Matthew 22:39

Giving yourself time, attention, and love during or after a divorce, may seem like an afterthought. Shifting your love, time, and attention to yourself is vital to your healing and growth after divorce. There is no one more important than you. Everything flows from you and if you are not intentionally loving and caring for yourself, you cannot properly give love to those that you love and care about.

Self-love is not selfish. Selfishness is about hurting others. Loving yourself simply requires that you be intentionally focusing on your needs. Divorce is a tough transition that requires you to be in good physical condition, well-rested, de-stressed, emotionally stable, and having a clear mind.

Whatever you need to acquire those things, should take priority.

1. When you think of self-love, what comes to your mind?

_____
_____
_____
_____
_____

2. Have you been focusing on self-love as a part of your divorce recovery? Why or why not?

_____
_____
_____
_____
_____
_____
_____

NOTES

12. Detecting Red Flags in Relationships

"The red flags are usually there you just have to keep your eyes open wider than your heart."
— April Mae Monterrosa

When you first meet that special someone and are getting to know them, both of you are putting your best foot forward. Asking a lot of questions during this time is a great way to get to understand another individual and to pick up on any inconsistencies or troubling behaviors. Unfortunately, many times in past relationships you may have recognized inconsistencies or negative behaviors, but still did not address them. Oftentimes, down the road in the relationship, those negative behaviors may grow or exacerbate because they were not questioned or challenged. As you look back, it is important to ask yourself why you chose not to ask more questions or address the negative behavior. This is important to understand, because left unaddressed, your same behavior or inability to address negative behaviors can show up in future relationships and give you similar results.

1. Did you notice any red flags in your former relationship prior to getting married? What were they?

   _____

   _____

2. Did you address the issues at all? If not, why did you choose not to address the negative issues?

   _____

   _____

   _____

NOTES

13. What is Your Next Step?

"You can fly as high as your belief will permit. Dream big. Believe bigger."

One of the most important aspects of divorce recovery is envisioning who you want to become and what you want to have in your new life. Once you have a vision, you can begin to take the steps to move in that direction.

Be patient with yourself during this process. Change does not happen overnight. You must be intentional and believe in your abilities to see your vision happen. With proper clarity and planning, you can take one small step at a time. Before you know it, you will begin to grow and change in different areas of your life.

Divorce is not the end of your life. God still loves you and will give you the desires of your heart. Keep believing in yourself and your ability to act towards the new life that you desire.

1. What areas of your emotional health do you need to change? Are you holding on to anger? Are you a people pleaser? Are you carrying around guilt or shame? If you are, what

resources can you find to help you overcome those challenges?

2. What areas of your external life would you like to change? What is one small step that you can make to move in that direction?

NOTES

14. Mask off!

"I am not free while any woman is unfree, even when her shackles are very different from my own."

-Audre Lorde

Freedom is the power or right to act, speak, or think as one wants without hindrance or restraint.

If you are not acting, speaking, or thinking for yourself, you may be showing up every day wearing a proverbial mask to appease others. It is time to learn to embrace who you truly are. No longer do you have to pretend to be someone that you are not. Everything about you is great and you must believe that. Even your flaws are beautifully and uniquely yours. You can choose every day to be authentically you.

1. After going through a separation or divorce, do you feel that you are wearing a mask at times? Why?

_____
_____
_____
_____
_____

2. What area of your life do you desire to be more authentically you?

_____

_____

_____

3. What are three things that you can do to begin to show up as your authentic self? (They can be internal or external attributes.)

_____

_____

_____

_____

_____

NOTES

15. A Victim No More!

"Never be bullied into silence. Never allow yourself to be made a victim. Accept no one's definition of your life; define yourself." -Harvey Fierstein

During the breakdown of a marriage, people are betrayed and hurt by the person who is supposed to love them. It can be extremely hurtful and challenging to move beyond any pain of that type of betrayal.

Even after a betrayal, you get to choose your perspective and behavior. Will you be a victim or a victor?

3. Take time to identify the betrayal, acknowledge your hurt, and decide to forgive and move forward. This is your life and your journey. Your choices will affect you, not the person who has betrayed you. You can only control your behavior and choices.

Who is the person who hurt you or betrayed you?

What happened?

What did you learn from the betrayal?

Are you ready to let go of what you can not change, and embrace the future that you can?

NOTES

16. Who Will You Become?

"It doesn't matter what has happened, all that matters is what's going to happen." -Bishop Daniel Robertson Jr.

Past marriages and relationships are a part of your history. You cannot change the past, but you can determine what you want, who you will become and create your future life. You have the power inside of you.

Will it be easy? NO. Is it too late? No. There is so much more life for you to live. Make a decision, plan, and then execute.

What personal characteristics do you want to have within yourself? Close your eyes and envision yourself with those characteristics. What does it feel like? What do you look like?

_____
_____
_____
_____

What are some tangible aspects that you desire in your life?

_____
_____
_____

NOTES

17. Do you know your value?

"Never chase love, affection, or attention. If it is not freely given by another person, it isn't worth having."

Going through a divorce or coming out of a long-term relationship, can leave you feeling lonely, unworthy and with low self-esteem. You may feel like you have lost pieces of your life. The truth is that you have not lost yourself. You are still there for yourself and remember, you are your most valuable asset.

As you navigate this new season of life, remember how precious and valuable you are. You do not have to settle for less in any area of your new life.

Take a moment to reflect and think about what you really want and need in your next romantic relationship. There is no right or wrong.

List your top 3-5 wants and needs:
1.___
2.___
3.___
4.___
5.___

NOTES

18. Adjust your focus.

"It is only in our darkest moments that we must focus to see the light." -Aristotle

The past has gone. No matter how challenging or tumultuous it was, you cannot change it. As you begin to heal, it is important to set your eyes on the future. Spend time with God, submit you hurt, pain and desires to Him. Be still and listen. You will receive a sense of peace and divine direction.

Focus on what is ahead of you. Do not look back because you are not going that way.

Take in a deep breath, hold for 3 seconds, and exhale. Do this three times.

What is on your heart, mind, and spirit today? What are your concerns?

_____
_____
_____
_____
_____

NOTES
_____

19. Are you ready to trust again?

"Trust yourself. Create the kind of self that you will be happy to live with all your life. Make the most of yourself by fanning the tiny, inner sparks of possibility into flames of achievement." –Golda Meir

Trusting someone else again after a separation or divorce can be quite a challenge to overcome. The truth of the matter is that you do not trust others, because we really do not trust yourself. Essentially, your thoughts are saying "I don't trust anyone else enough to take care of me." Taking care of you may be taking care of your emotions, taking care of you physically or financially. You must first trust yourself enough to take good care of yourself. When you are taking care of your mind, body, spirit, and finances, you have less of a reliance or concern about entrusting those areas of your life to someone else because you ultimately control those areas.

1. Do you trust yourself? Why or why not?

   _____

   _____

2. What area of your life do you feel highly competent and trusting of yourself?

   _____

   _____

3. What makes you feel a high level of competence in that area?

   _____

   _____

   _____

   _____

   _____

4. Which areas of your life do you not trust yourself? Why do you believe you lack trust in those areas?

_____

_____

_____

_____

5. What similar ways can you channel energy from your competencies to the areas of your life where you lack trust in yourself?

_____

_____

_____

NOTES
_____

20. The Coparenting Blues

"No matter how you feel about your ex, try your best to be peaceful. Hold space for your child to love you both without guilt." -Hayley Gallagher

Seeing your ex on a regular basis to exchange your children can be emotionally frustrating on many levels. However, regardless of your current feelings and relationship with your ex, it is important to think about your children, look beyond the now and begin this coparenting journey with the end in mind.

Take a moment to think ahead and envision your child and their other parent 10 years from now.
Will they be a teenager? Will they be a young adult?

How will your child benefit from having a healthy relationship with the other parent in that season of their lives?

Though you may not like the other parent right now. Though you may have been hurt by the other parent and are incredibly angry at them, you must temporarily put those emotions aside when it comes to making decisions in the best interest of your children. As time passes and you begin to heal and further move on with your life, your coparenting challenges will lessen if you adhere to a few quick rules.

1. Keep all communication on topics that are directly related to the children. No more and no less.
2. Do not ask your children questions about the other parent's actions or personal business. Be mature enough to peacefully contact them and

ask any pertinent questions or concerns that you may have.

3. Utilize text and email as much as possible to eliminate emotion related calls and escalations especially during the early stages of co-parenting.

4. Find a public place to meet and exchange the children. Try to use a half-way point. This keeps the adults out of each other's personal space and dwellings.

5. Unless you truly feel that your children are in danger, (in which you will need to call the authorities) allow the other parent to parent their way. Ideally, you should eventually be able to communicate and collaborate on common goals. However, it is more important that the children have time with their parents, vs "perfect parenting."

Write down your desired vision of your children and the other parent in 10 years.

What would that relationship look like?

Why would both parents be important in the children's lives at that time?

What actions can you change right now to assist in that future vision?

_____

_____

_____

_____

_____

_____

_____

NOTES
_____

21. Some things must go.

"I will attract only happiness the moment I release all resentment."-J.R. Incer,

Do you feel heavy and weighted down at times? Do you find yourself replaying the negative experiences that you had with your ex in your mind? Do you feel sluggish in your physical body no matter what you seem to do? Are you constantly having negative conversations about your ex with family and friends?

If you have ever been hurt or betrayed in a relationship, then you know that you may be carrying a host of negative emotions. Perhaps it is time for you to release them so that you can begin to feel the joy and energy that you once knew. Holding on to negative, toxic emotions like anger, hate, and vengeance that are not released, can prevent you from moving into a new happy life.

Assess your feelings right now.

What type of emotional state do you feel most of the time?

Who has hurt you in the past?

How do you feel about the person who has hurt?

Write a letter to that individual expressing your former thoughts and feelings as well as your current thoughts and feelings. Get all those feelings out on paper. Once you have completed it, you can burn it, tear it up, or flush it.

Let it all go.

_____

_____

_____

_____

NOTES

22. Rejection is real.

"Rejection is merely a redirection; A course correction to your destiny." -Uknown

If you have experienced any type of rejection in your marriage, relationships, or within your family, there may be a residue of feelings of rejection hanging on in your life. In a marriage, rejection may come through abuse, betrayal, and infidelity. As human beings, we desire to be accepted, loved, valued, and received. When we feel otherwise, the feelings of feeling unwanted, unappreciated, and abandoned, can take up residence in your emotions. Feeling rejected can cause bitterness, anger, depression, negative thinking patterns, people pleasing along with a host of other characteristics.
If you have ever felt rejected, know that your feelings are valid and that through prayer and the breaking of

old thought patterns and negative core beliefs, healing can be restored.

Have you ever been rejected?

_____

What was the worst thought or feeling about that rejection?

_____

_____

Is your life currently still affected by that rejection? If so, in what way?

_____

_____

_____

_____

NOTES
_____

23. Loneliness vs Singleness

"Loneliness expresses the pain of being alone and solitude expresses the glory of being alone."

–Paul Tillich

After divorce, dealing with loneliness is a common fear of divorcées. Being alone and being lonely are two very different things. Being alone is a state if being. You may be alone in your car or in your office. However, loneliness is an emotional feeling or response to a situation or circumstance.

As a divorcée, finding yourself alone often is an adjustment that will eventually become your new norm. I had to go through the very same transition after a 13 - year marriage. It takes time but it is very doable.

Here are 3 tips that can help you begin to combat the feeling of loneliness:

1. Find a new hobby, interest, or opportunity to serve. What have you been wanting to do for a very long time? Maybe you have wanted to go back to school, learn to knit, run, cycle, travel, join an organization or cause. Learning something new gives you a new focus, activity, and excitement. If you've ever had a cause that is dear to your heart, now is the time to get involved and focus your energies on those who need your help.

2. Shift your focus. Stop focusing on the past negativity and begin to look ahead at an opportunity for new life beginnings. Your perspective becomes your reality.

3. Find an awesome support system. Be around people who love and support you and have your best interest in

mind. Do not do divorce alone. Create an atmosphere of positive people. Meet new friends and acquaintances. The key here is to be intentional about loneliness before loneliness shows up.

List 3 activities that you have always wanted to explore or rekindle.

- _____
- _____
- _____

List a 2 causes or community projects that have been dear to you heart.

- _____
- _____

NOTES

24. Fighting Forgiveness

"Forgiveness is a gift that you give yourself."

Forgiveness is a challenge for many divorcées. When someone has hurt you, it can be very difficult to forgive them. The challenge is that holding on to the hurt and anger only weighs you down, and the longer that you hold on to the hurt, the harder it is to let go. You can release anger and find forgiveness through prayer.

<u>The Prayer of Forgiveness</u>

Prayer of Forgiveness Father, in the name of Jesus, I make a fresh commitment to You to live in peace and harmony. I let go of all anger, bitterness, resentment, guilt, and shame. I give no place to the enemy, in the name of Jesus. Father, I ask Your forgiveness for any wrongdoing, by faith, I receive it, having assurance that

I am cleansed from all unrighteousness through Jesus Christ. Now Father, I ask You to forgive and release all who have wronged and hurt me. I forgive and release them. Deal with them in your mercy and kindness. From this moment on, I purpose to walk in love and peace. I know that I have right standing with You and that You hear my prayers. I will continue to praise you. In Jesus' name. Amen

Thoughts:

_____

_____

_____

_____

_____

25. The Angst of Anger

"Holding on to anger, resentment, and hurt only gives you tense muscles, a headache, and a sore jaw from clenching your teeth. Forgiveness gives you back the laughter and the lightness in your life."

-Joan Lunden

Anger is an honest emotion to feel during and after a divorce. Anger is not good or bad, it is an emotion. However, left unexpressed outwardly, it will process inwardly in a variety of ways. Releasing anger frees your mind, body, and spirit and brings the much-needed clarity for your new life's journey.

Here are a few healthy ways to begin to release your anger:

1. Write out exactly what you are angry about or even write a letter to the person with whom you are angry with. When complete, you can rip it up, burn it or flush it.
2. Take time alone and cry, scream, yell, hit a few pillows. Seriously, just get it out without hurting or harming anyone else. This is a solo act.
3. Run, walk, exercise, or hit some baseballs or golf balls. Release that anger through physical activity.

The key here is to release those feelings. It is okay. Many people have been walking around with "divorce" anger for decades. Holding on to anger has made them miserable, unhappy, edgy, moody, and feeling like a ticking time bomb. That does not have to be you.

The choice is always yours. You can be free from the anger of past events so that you can begin an authentic healing process. You deserve that.

NOTES

---

26. The Will to be Well

"The greatest wealth is health."

"Do you not know that your bodies are temples of the Holy Spirit, who is in you, whom you have received from God? You are not your own;"

- 1 Cor 6:19

Wellness consists of making sure your body is working at its optimum ability. This is extremely vital during your divorce journey. Divorce challenges every aspect of your well-being. It challenges your physical body, your emotional stability, your financial wellness, your spiritual connection, and your social interactions.

Among the obvious things such as eating well, getting enough exercise and adequate amounts of sleep, it also entails the more uncomfortable aspects of physical and emotional health that you may not feel comfortable about, like going to the doctor for a physical, seeing a therapist, coach, or counselor, and going to the dentist.

You are your most important asset. Make a commitment to care for your *overall* wellness. Take a few moments and schedule the following within the next three months.

- Annual Physical Exam

  _____

- Consultation for a therapist, coach, or counselor.

  _____

- Dental checkup

  _____

NOTES

27. Your Mindset Matters

"Finally, brothers, whatever is true, whatever is noble, whatever is right, whatever is pure, whatever is lovely, whatever is admirable–if anything is excellent or praiseworthy–think about such things." -Phillipians 4:8

God never performs His greatest feats in your yesterdays. Regardless of your past, God has amazing things in store for you in your life. Regardless of what someone may have said about you, regardless of the way someone may have mistreated you, God is in the business of restoration. Divorce hurts. Divorce breaks pieces of you, but God can put you back together, piece by piece, day by day.

Focus your mind on your future. There is not anything that you cannot accomplish with hard work and God on your side. He is restoring a new life for you, He is repairing your heart, and He is continuing to equip you with everything necessary for the desires and goals in your heart. You must know that with every fiber of your being.

God has great things in store for you today, and the days to come. Keep your mind focused on the things that you are grateful for and keep moving forward into your greatness.

What are you grateful for on today?

_____

_____

_____

_____

_____

NOTES
_____

28. Check your environment.

"Tell me with whom you associate, and I will tell you who you are."

-Johann Wolfgang von Goethe

It is a great day to look around your environment.
Who is in it?
What was the last conversation that you had?

Your association has a great deal to do with how you manage your divorce journey. I am going to be frank. It is vital that you keep as many positive and uplifting people around you as possible.

There is nothing that will drag you back to step one quicker than someone who is negative, encouraging a pity party, or focusing on vengeance or anger. Even if it is a family member, their communication should be limited.

Sound harsh? Nope. Remember, this is your life and your journey, and you will need to set boundaries to keep you moving forward.

In addition, read positive books, listen to positive uplifting music, limit the news, and negative social media. Look and listen today. Pay attention to what is around you and monitor your feelings and emotions. You may need to make a few changes in your environment to move peacefully into the next chapter of your life.

What area of your environment are you willing to change and make more positive?

_____

_____

_____

NOTES
_____

29. Fostering New Friendships

"Friendship is born at that moment when one person says to another, 'What you too? I thought I was the only one.'"- C.S. Lewis

During or after a divorce, friendships can change and that is a normal part of the divorce journey. Oftentimes, friendships are created due to commonalities. Those commonalities can be spouses, children, in-laws, communities, and work environments. The transitions and changes of a divorce can impact the nature of relationships both emotionally and logistically. Though it can be a great loss at times, it is an opportunity to meet and establish new acquaintances and friends with similar interests and lifestyles. This shift may require effort on your part to embrace new opportunities to meet new people. Have fun exploring new activities and new environments.

Have you experienced any changes is your friendships? List the commonalities that brought you and those friends together.

_____

_____

_____

Do you think you can salvage any friendships that have been strained during the divorce? Why or why not?

_____

_____

_____

_____

_____

NOTES

_____

30. Acceptance, the Final Frontier

"Therefore, if anyone is in Christ, he is a new creation. The old is passed away; behold, the new has come." -2 Corinthians 5:17

Finally gaining acceptance of your divorce is the goal of divorce recovery. It is one of the major healing goals of such a major life transition. At this juncture your emotions have stabilized, and you are living in the reality of the present.

There are still both good and not so good days, however you are able to manage your emotions and are focusing more on the future than on the past. You are beginning to gain a sense of a new normal and are embracing your new experiences.

Getting to a level of acceptance requires navigating a mirage of feelings along the way. Guilt, shame, anger, sadness, and fear are all a part of the journey. Be patient with yourself and your process. You will know when you get to a level of acceptance, by how peacefully and unaffected you respond to the details of the past.

Do you feel that you have reached the stage of acceptance? Why or why not?

_____

_____

_____

_____

Which negative emotions are you still feeling on a regular basis?

_____

_____

_____

_____

What will it take for you to release those negative emotions?

_____

_____

_____

_____

_____

NOTES
_____

Appendix

Prayer of Forgiveness

Prayer of Forgiveness Father, in the name of Jesus, I make a fresh commitment to You to live in peace and harmony. I let go of all anger, bitterness, resentment, guilt, and shame. I give no place to the enemy, in the name of Jesus. Father, I ask Your forgiveness for any wrongdoing, by faith, I receive it, having assurance that I am cleansed from all unrighteousness through Jesus Christ. Now Father, I ask You to forgive and release all who have wronged and hurt me. I forgive and release them. Deal with them in your mercy and kindness. From this moment on, I purpose to walk in love and peace. I know that I have right standing with You and that You hear my prayers. I will continue to praise you. In Jesus' name. Amen

Divorce Devotions: Healing for a Broken Heart

ABOUT THE AUTHOR

Andrea M. Stuckey is passionate about helping women through the devastating life changes that come along with separation and divorce. She is the Founder of Live Life Luvd Coaching LLC, Divorced Women Unite™ and the Divorce Liberator Podcast ™ where she is dedicated to helping women rebuild their lives through life-coaching, speaking, teaching and writing.

Andrea is also the author of several books including "Suddenly Single: A Woman's Spiritual and Practical Guide to the First 5 Years Following Separation and Divorce" and she is an Amazon Best Selling Author as well.

Coach Andrea teaches divorced women how to cultivate and activate their gifts and talents, in order to redefine their lives and pursue their personal goals and dreams.

Andrea is the mother to two adult children. Having gone through divorce twice, she empowers women, shares her journey, and gives spiritual and practical tips that are applicable to living a liberated lifestyle.

Stay connected with her at andreamstuckey.com

Made in the USA
Middletown, DE
06 September 2024